PERSON UNDER

PAIGE THOMAS

Finishing Line Press
Georgetown, Kentucky

PERSON UNDER

Copyright © 2026 by Paige Thomas
ISBN 979-8-89990-316-8 First Edition
All rights reserved under International and Pan-American Copyright Conventions. No part of this book may be reproduced in any manner whatsoever without written permission from the publisher, except in the case of brief quotations embodied in critical articles and reviews.

Publisher: Leah Huete de Maines
Editor: Christen Kincaid
Cover Art: Paige Thomas 2023
Author Photo: Rocco Weyer 2023
Cover Design: Paige Thomas 2025

Order online: www.finishinglinepress.com
also available on amazon.com

Author inquiries and mail orders:
Finishing Line Press
PO Box 1626
Georgetown, Kentucky 40324
USA

for Blair, Mum, and me

CONTENTS

NOTE xiii

I. _____ / DAUGHTER / SISTER

[Full Name] 2
[If Caregiver] 3
[Safety as] 4
[SKIP relationship] 5
[life plan?] 6
[begin again] 7
[Numb Numb] 8
[in the] 9

II. GUARDIAN / MOTHER / _____

[Say a] 12
[Old gun] 13
[you have] 14
[If success] 15
[eliminating self] 16
[Original opened] 17
[Say a] 18
[on brook] 19

III. WARD / DAUGHTER / SISTER

[who is] 22
[1 2 3] 23
[following Care] 24
[in a] 25
[and/or] 26
[O to] 27
[Is this] 28
[part Ward] 29

IV. MATERIALS

INTERVIEWS 33

GUARDIAN'S ANNUAL STATUS REPORT FOR AN ADULT.... 41

RAW MATERIALS 51

ACKNOWLEDGMENTS..53

BIO 55

"[A]n antelope running wild would not be a document, but an antelope taken into a zoo would be one…"

—*Paper Knowledge*, Lisa Gitelman

NOTE

Every year after my little sister turned eighteen, my mother has filed an eight-page document with the state of Idaho to remain my little sister's legal guardian. The official name of the form is "Guardian's Annual Status Report for An Adult," or that's what it was called the very first time my mother looked at it, brought me over to her, and asked if I could fill it out.

Person Under returns to that original document except now I am—and my mother and sister are—speaking how we couldn't before. Through erasure, an obscuring of a source text until it is transformed, the authority these eight pages has over my family is reimagined.

Informed by interviews with my mother and little sister and erased from each of our points of view, *Person Under* is made in service of possibility.

I

_____ / DAUGHTER / SISTER

Full Name _____

Mailing Address _____

City, State and Zip Code

Telephone _____

Email Address (if any) _____

IN THE DISTRICT COURT FOR THE _____ JUDICIAL DISTRICT
FOR THE STATE OF _____ AND FOR THE COUNTY OF _____

IN THE **MATTER OF** THE ESTATE OF:

Case No.

GUARDIAN'S ANNUAL STATUS REPORT
FOR AN ADULT

an Incapacitated Person

Fee Category: ___

x **an Individual with** a Developmental Disability

Fee Category: D4.2

Instructions.

This form provides the court with information about an incapacitated adult or individual with a developmental disability for whom a guardian has been appointed. This form should NOT be completed for a minor who has **a guardian**.

A guardian **must** file this report within 30 days of the anniversary of the guardian's appointment **and annually thereafter** or as otherwise ordered. Answer all applicable questions thoroughly. Type or write _____ make sure they are readable.

This report must be signed by the _____ filed with the court. Copies **must** be provided to the p_____ any other individuals specified by the court. Please r_____

WARD'S CURRENT RESIDENCE:

Ward's Phy...
Ward's Te...
Residen...
C...

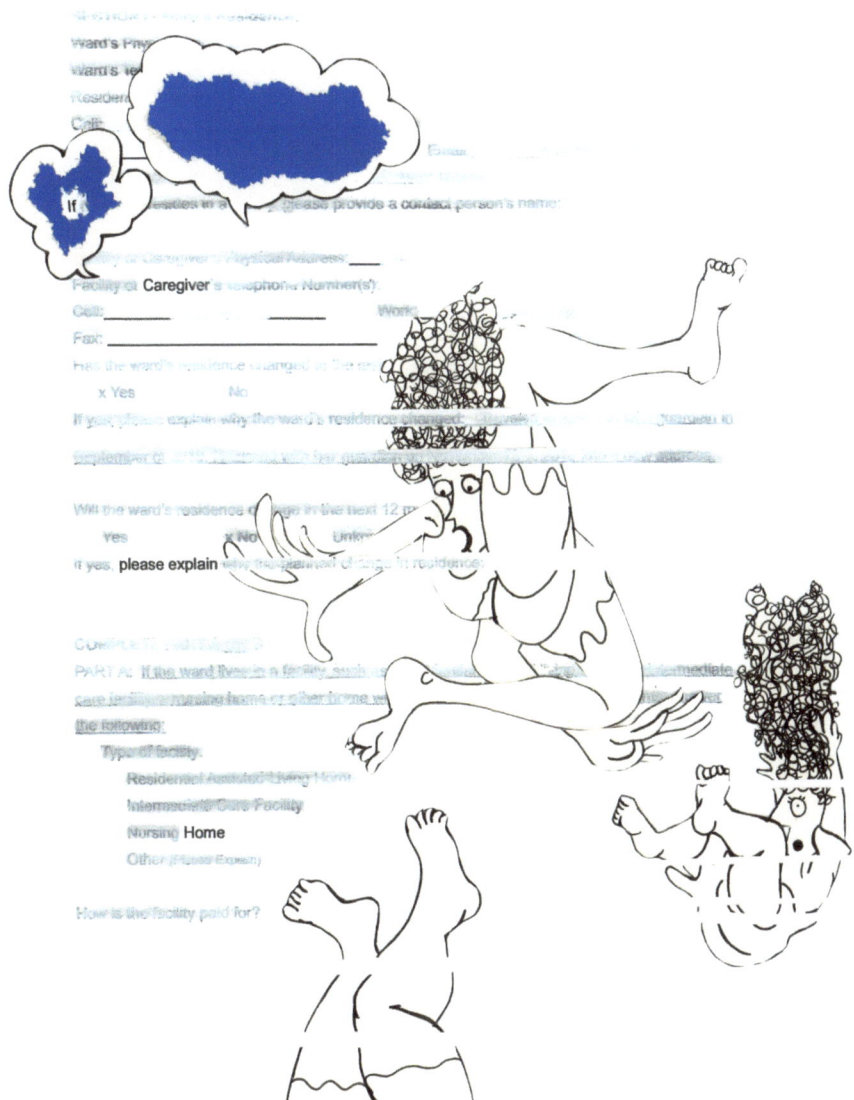

If ... resides in a ... please provide a contact person's name:

... of Caregiver's Physical Address: _____
Facility or **Caregiver**'s Telephone Number(s):
Cell: _____ Work: _____
Fax: _____

Has the ward's residence changed in the ...
  x Yes   No

If yes, please explain why the ward's residence changed: ...
September ... 2019, ... with her guardian ...

Will the ward's residence change in the next 12 m...
  Yes   x No   Unkn...

If yes, **please explain** why the ... change in residence:

COMPLETE THE FOLLOWING:
PART A: **If the ward lives in a facility**, such as ... intermediate care ... nursing home or other home ... the following:
  Type of facility:
    Residential Assisted Living Home
    Intermediate Care Facility
    Nursing **Home**
    Other (Please Explain)

How is the facility paid for?

Do you have any concerns regarding quality of care received by the ward in the following areas:

Cleanliness	No
Nutrition/Meals	No
Personal Care	No
Privacy	Yes
Individualized Care Plans	Yes
Safety	Yes

If you replied "yes", why is something please explain:

Describe any restrictions placed upon the ward in the facility, such as limiting visitors or phone calls:

Who imposed the restrictions and when were they imposed:

What are the reasons for the restrictions:

Describe why this facility was chosen for the ward:

Describe the ward's satisfaction with the placement:

Do you believe the ward could live and function in a less restrictive setting?   Yes   No
If yes, why?

If yes, have you tried to change the placement?

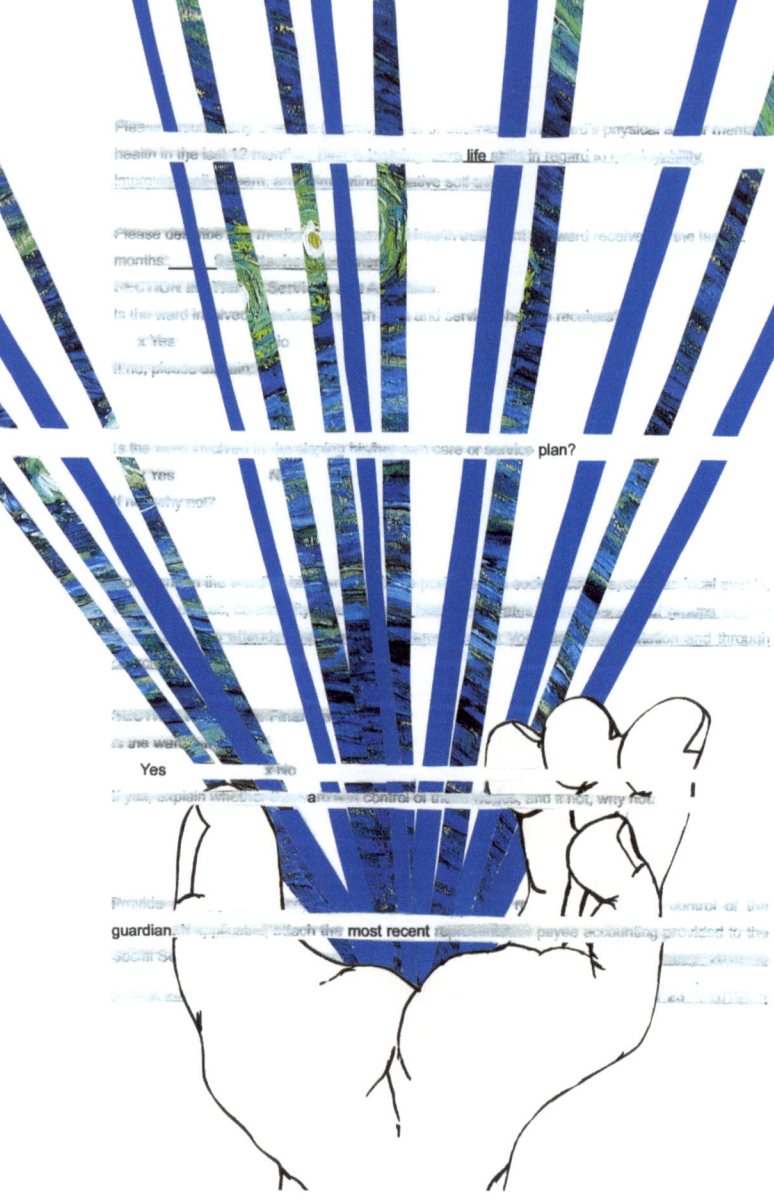

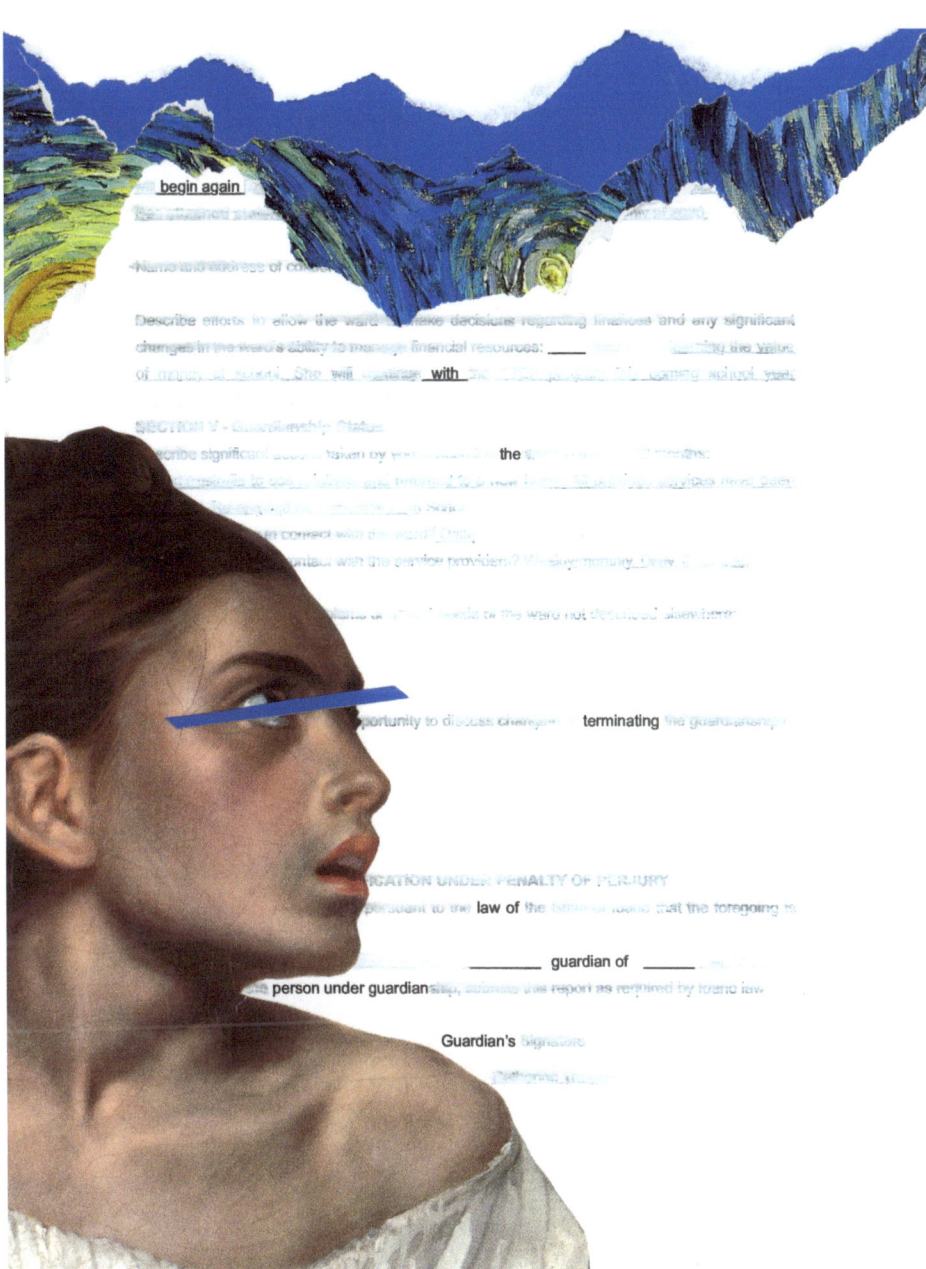

begin again

Name and address of co

Describe efforts to allow the ward to make decisions regarding finances and any significant changes in the ward's ability to manage financial resources: ____ **with**

SECTION V - Guardianship Status

the

terminating

law of

_____ **guardian of** _____

person under guardian

Guardian's

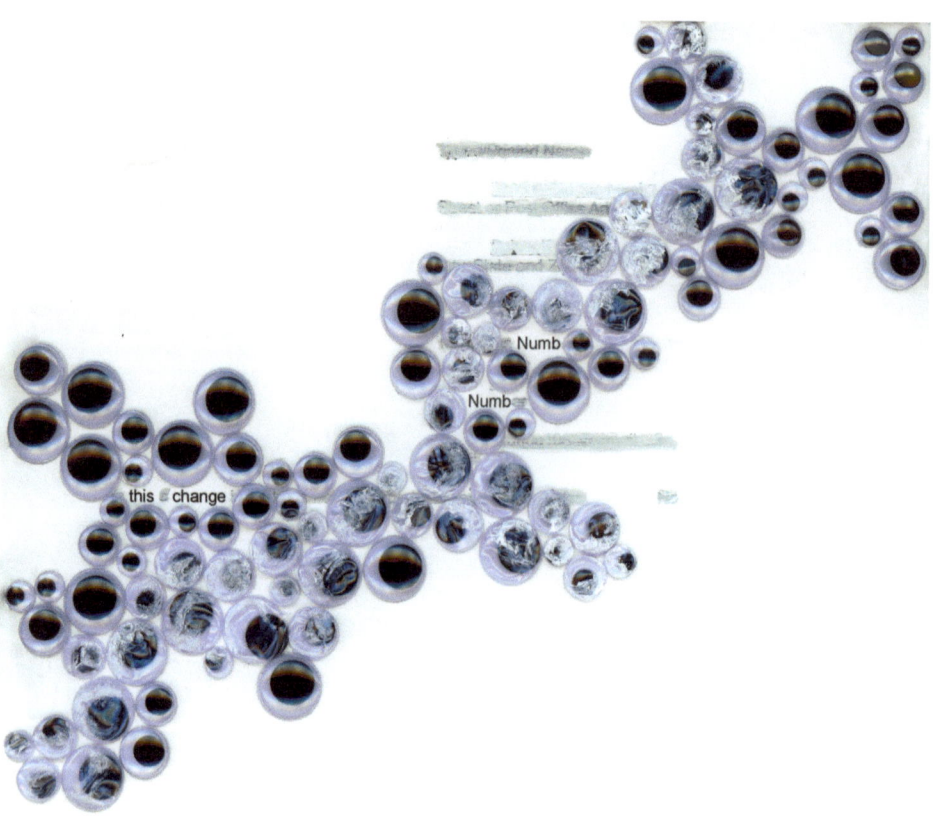

CERTIFICATE OF SERVICE

I certify that on (date) _____ I served a copy (to) (name) all parties in the case other than yourself):

x Ward:
                                                    x By mail
                                                    x By fax number
                                                    x By personal delivery
                                                    x Overnight delivery/Fed Ex

x Ward's attorney (name and address):
                                                    x By mail
                                                    x By fax (number)
                                                    x By personal delivery
                                                    x Overnight delivery/Fed Ex

x Person(s) designated by court order
   (name and address):
                                                    x By mail
                                                    x By fax (number)
                                                    x By personal delivery
                                                    x Overnight delivery/Fed Ex

x Others (name and address):
        River
                                                    x By mail
                                                    x By fax number
                                                    x By personal delivery
                                                    x Overnight delivery

Type/Printed name   Guardian's Signature

II

GUARDIAN / MOTHER / _____

SECTION 1 - Ward's Residence.
Ward's Physical Address: _____ Old _____
Ward's Telephone Number(s):
Residence.
Cell _____ Work _____
_____ gun _____
_____ of _____ Caregiver. _____
If the ward resides in a facility, please provide a contact person's name.

Facility or Caregiver's Physical Address: _____
Facility or Caregiver's Telephone Number(s):
Cell _____ Work _____
Fax _____ Email _____
Has the ward's residence changed in the last 12 months?
　　x Yes　　　　　No

If yes, please explain why the ward's residence changed. _____ led to _____ new guardian. September _____ issued with her guardianship file _____ in to a new address.

Will the ward's residence change in the next 12 months?
　　Yes　　　x No　　　Unknown

If yes, please explain in why the planned change in residence.

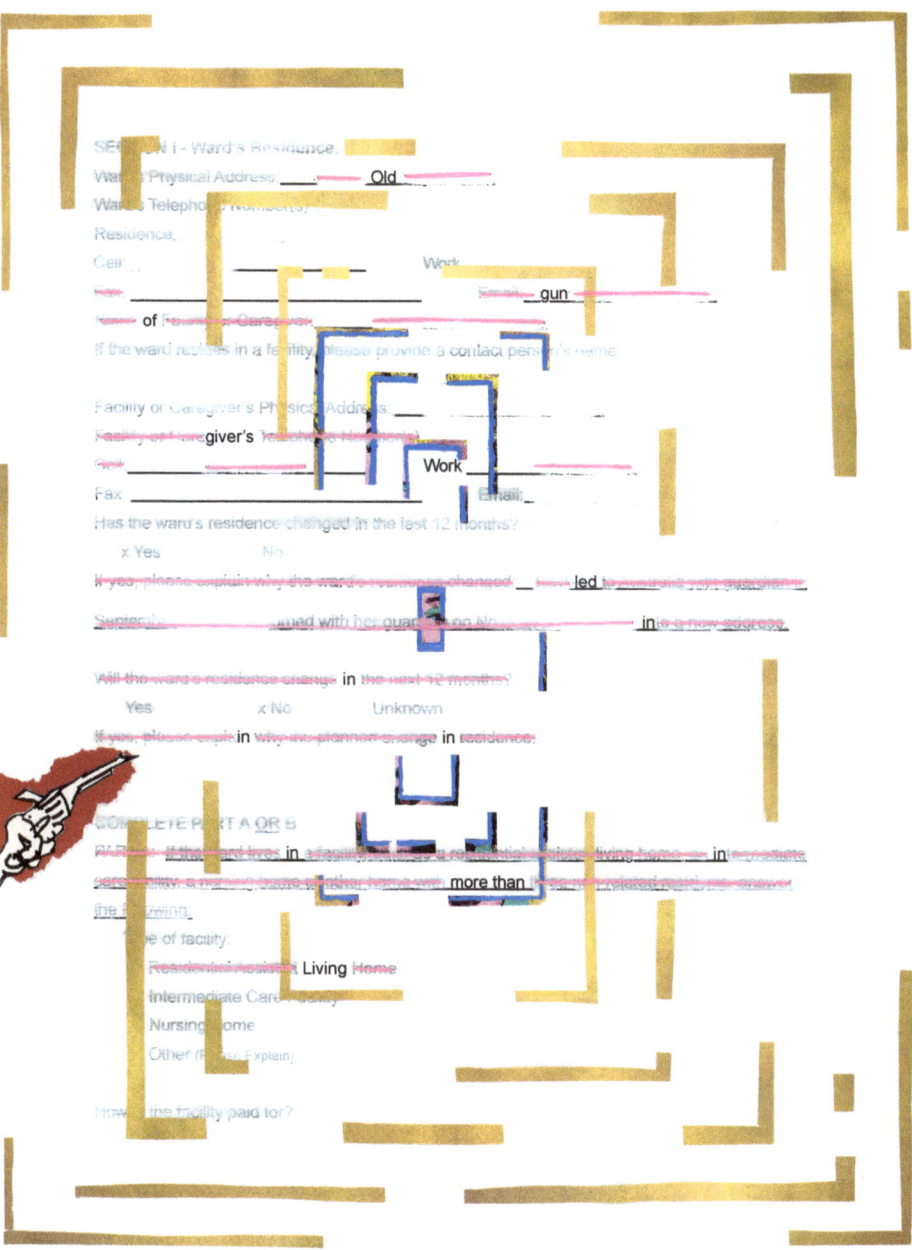

COMPLETE PART A OR B
PART A: If the ward lives in a facility, such as a residential assisted living home, in a private care facility, a nursing home or other home with more than _____ unrelated people, please answer the following:
Type of facility:
　　Residential Assisted Living Home
　　Intermediate Care Facility
　　Nursing Home
　　Other (Please Explain)

How is the facility paid for?

you have concerns

Cleanliness	Yes	No
Nutrition/Meals	Yes	No
Personal Care	Yes	No
Privacy	Yes	No
Individualized Care Plans	Yes	No
Safety	Yes	No

marked

upon the ward

strict

you believe

setting?   Yes   No
If yes, why?

you tried to

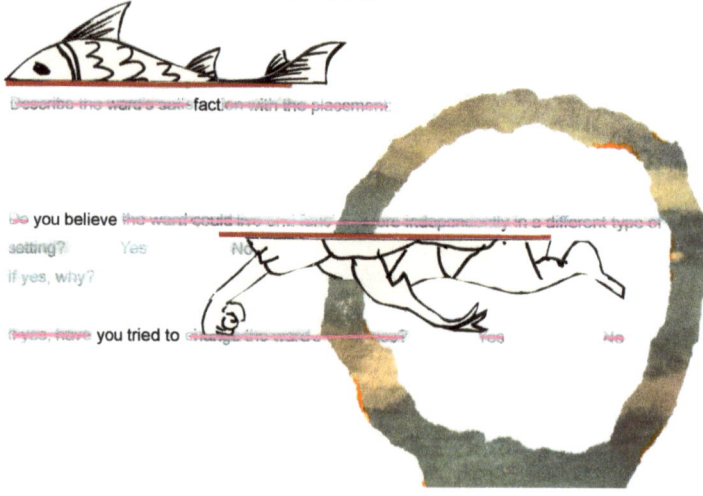

If ~~y........~~ success ~~.........~~

SKIP TO SECTION II
~~..........~~ does not live ~~..................................~~
~~..........~~ in the ~~..................................~~
mother
~~..........~~ who moved ~~..................~~. _____

~~..........~~ the ward's ~~..................................~~
~~..........~~ the source ~~..........~~:
Name: _____ ___ _____ Relationship to ward: _____ ___
~~Dates of Services:~~ n/a
Monthly Payment: _____ n/a _____ Source of Payment: _____ n/a

Does the ward live with a convicted felon?
    Yes   x No   Unknown
If yes, please explain:

SECTION II – Ward's Health
Please describe the ward's current physical health:
   ~~...~~ or   ~~...~~   ~~...~~   ~~excellent~~
If poor, please explain:

~~..........~~ the ~~..................~~
~~..........~~ ~~..........~~ ~~..........~~ cell~~.~~
If poor, please explain:

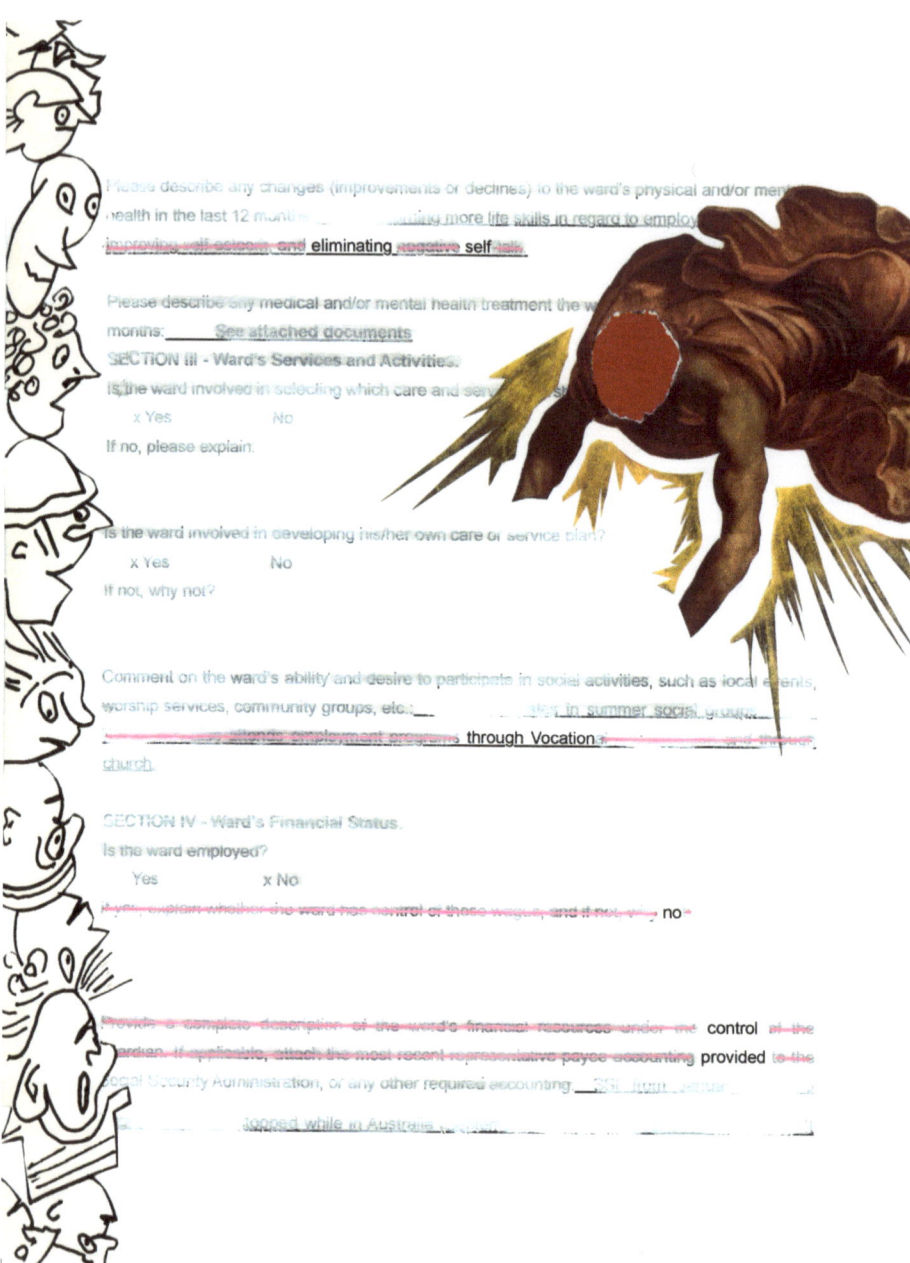

Please describe any changes (improvements or declines) to the ward's physical and/or mental health in the last 12 months ~~learning~~ more life skills in regard to employ~~ment~~ ~~improving self-esteem, and~~ eliminating ~~negative~~ self ~~talk.~~

Please describe ~~any~~ medical and/or mental health treatment the w~~ard~~ months: See attached documents

SECTION III - Ward's Services and Activities.

Is the ward involved in selecting which care and serv~~ices~~ ~~~~
   x Yes   No

If no, please explain.

Is the ward involved in developing his/her own care or service plan?
   x Yes   No

If not, why not?

Comment on the ward's ability and desire to participate in social activities, such as local events, worship services, community groups, etc. ~~~~ ~~~~ in summer social group ~~~~ ~~attends employment programs~~ through Vocation ~~~~ ~~and the~~ church.

SECTION IV - Ward's Financial Status.

Is the ward employed?
   Yes   x No

~~If yes, explain whether the ward has control of those wages, and if not, why.~~ no

~~Provide a complete description of the ward's financial resources under the~~ control ~~of the guardian. If applicable, attach the most recent representative payee accounting~~ provided ~~to the Social Security Administration, or any other required accounting.~~ ~~SSI from Jesus~~ ~~~~ ~~stopped while in Australia~~ ~~~~

will begin again in _____ Original account funds were put into guardian's account. See attached statements. New account to be opened in ward's name.

Name and address of conservator, if any: ___n/a___

Describe efforts to allow the ward to make decisions regarding finances and any significant changes in the ward's ability to manage financial resources: _____ is learning the value of money at school. She will continue with the _____ program this coming school year.

SECTION V - Guardianship Status:
Describe significant actions taken by you concerning the ward in the last 12 months:
Visited Australia to see relatives and returned to a new home. All previous services have been reinstated and enrolled in

How often are you in contact with the ward? Daily
How often are you in contact with the service providers? frequently, as a parent needed

Describe any significant problems or unmet needs of the ward, of other concerns?
n/a

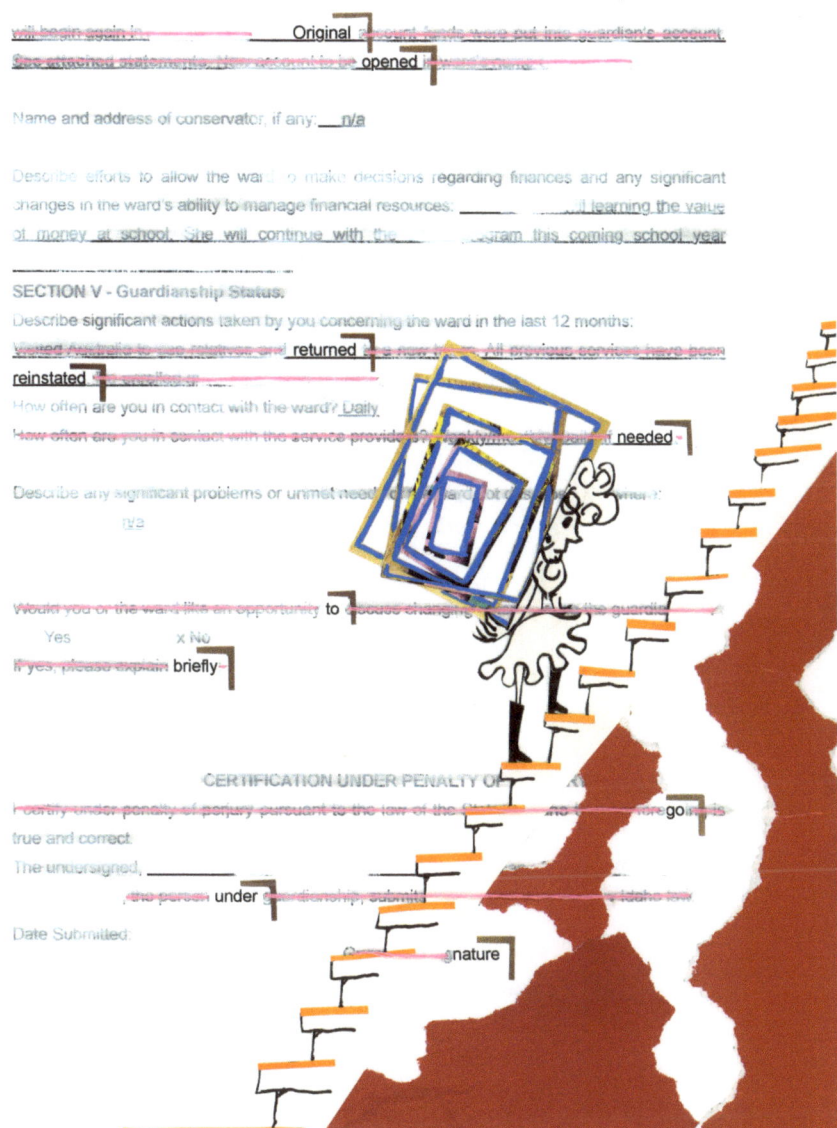

Would you or the ward like an opportunity to discuss changing or ending the guardianship?
    Yes   x No
If yes, please explain briefly

CERTIFICATION UNDER PENALTY OF PERJURY
I certify under penalty of perjury pursuant to the law of the State of Idaho that foregoing is true and correct.
The undersigned, _____, _____, the person under guardianship, submits _____ Idaho law

Date Submitted: _____   _____ Signature

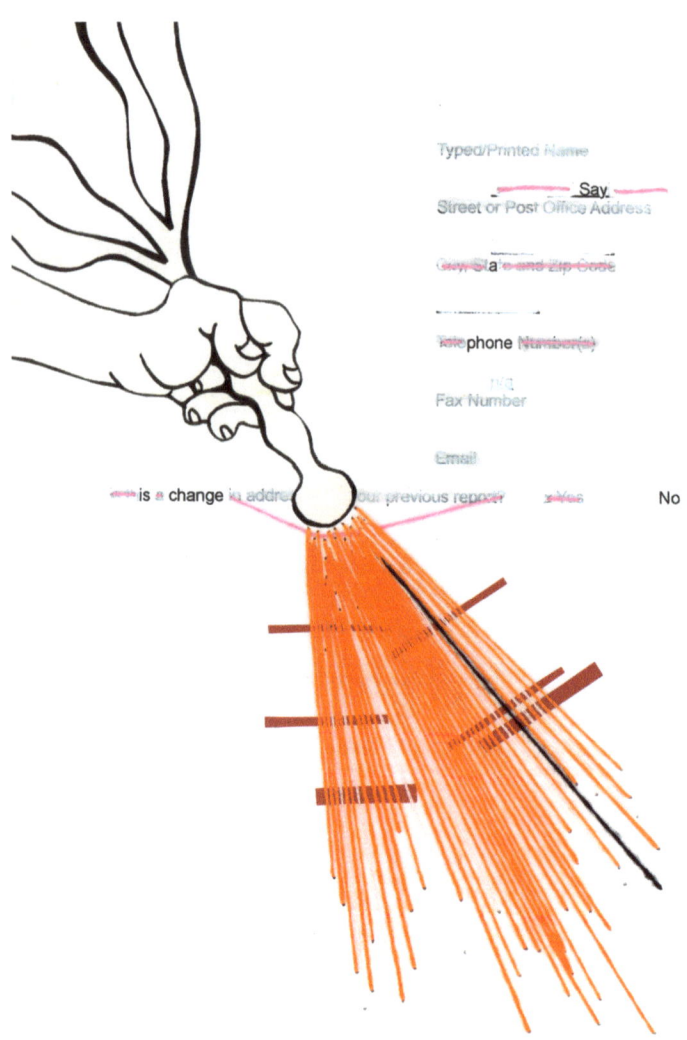

CERTIFICATE OF SERVICE

_____ on (date) _____ served a copy to: (name all parties in the case other than yourself)

x Ward:
   _____/brook_____
                                    X By mail
                                    X By fax (number)
                                    X By personal delivery
                                    X Overnight delivery/Fed Ex

x Ward's attorney (name and address):
                                    X By mail
                                    X By fax (number)
                                    X By personal delivery
                                    X Overnight delivery/Fed Ex

   Person(s)/designated by court order
   (name and address):
                                    X By mail
                                    X By fax (number)
                                    X By personal delivery
                                    X Overnight delivery/Fed Ex

x Others (name and address):
                                    X By mail
                                    X By fax (number)
                                    X By personal delivery
                                    X Overnight delivery/Fed Ex

_____ Typed/printed name _____   _____ Guardian's signature _____

III

WARD / DAUGHTER / SISTER

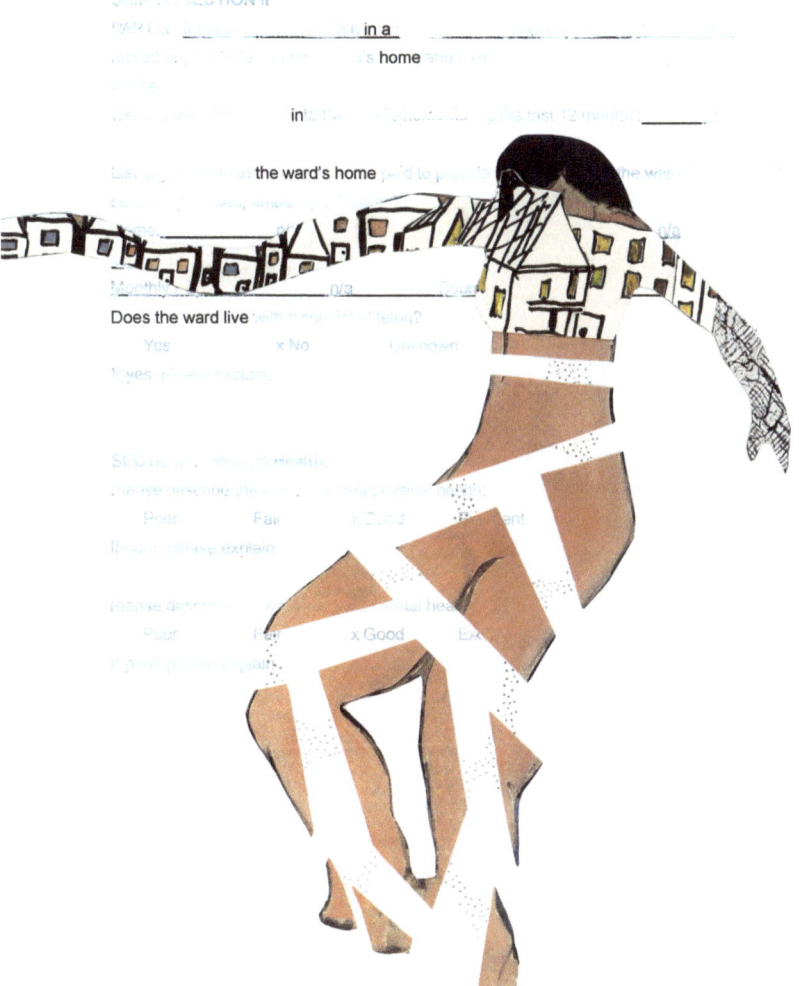

If yes, was the change a success? If not, why not?

SKIP TO SECTION II

PART I: in a
                                                's home

                            into the   the last 12 months

List   the ward's home   the w
B

Monthly   n/a

Does the ward live   ?
    Yes   x No
If yes,   .

SECTION   Health
Please describe
    Poor   Fair   x Good   Excellent
If   explain

Please describe   health
    Poor   Fair   x Good   Excellent
If   explain

Is this   from you   ?

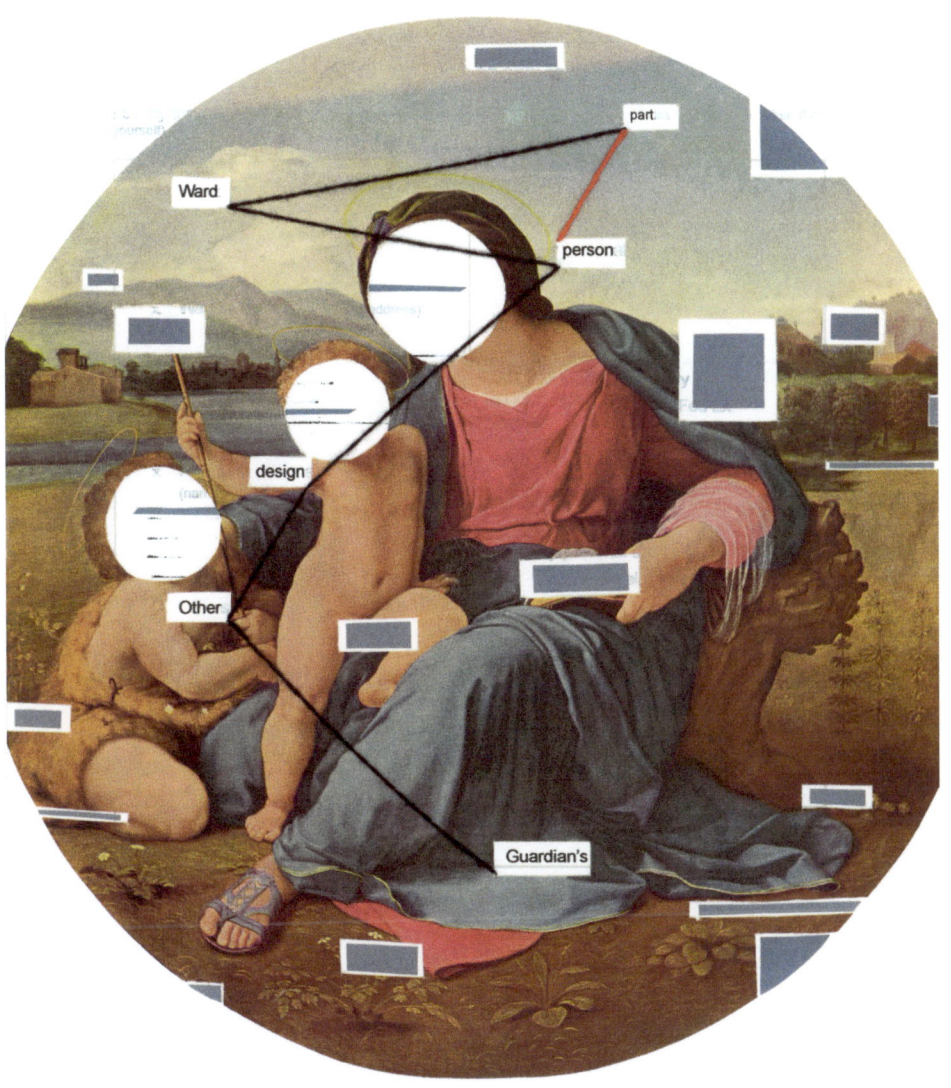

IV

MATERIALS

INTERVIEWS

_____ / DAUGHTER / SISTER

ASSOCIATION / WORD / COLOR

What is authority?	tradition	red
What is choice?	agency	white
What is care?	presence	dark green
What is obligation?	mandatory	silver
What is motherhood?	overcome	amber
What is permanence?	sightless	fuchsia
What is morning?	new	blush
What is law?	failure	black
What is disability?	divergence	sky blue
What is love?	warmth	maroon
What is the past?	gone	gray
What is adulthood?	driving	yellow
What is a year?	repetition	rust
What is home?	found	gold
What is daughter?	render	lilac
What is belief?	persistence	black
What is rest?	unburden	cream
What is protection?	cover up	pink
What is ending?	no more	red
What is legacy?	what's left	brown
What is grief?	burning	violet
What is the future?	unknown	white
	apology	blue

GUARDIAN / MOTHER / _____

ASSOCIATION / WORD / COLOR

What is authority?	discipline	red
What is choice?	right/wrong	grey
What is care?	soft	pink
What is obligation?	debt	white
What is motherhood?	a mountain	pink
What is permanence?	cement	green
What is morning?	sunshine	yellow
What is law?	penalty	black
What is disability?	wheelchair	purple
What is love?	heart	pink
What is the past?	gray	brown
What is adulthood?	fear	dark blue
What is a year?	annual	blue
What is home?	warm	green
What is daughter?	love	pink
What is belief?	religion	emerald green
What is rest?	peace	light blue
What is protection?	armor	dark brown
What is ending?	death	black
What is legacy?	memories	purple
What is grief?	sadness	black
What is the future?	fruitful	white
	loneliness	orange

WARD / DAUGHTER / SISTER

ASSOCIATION / WORD / COLOR

What is authority?	truth	red
What is choice?	good	blue
What is family?	great	purple
What is routine?	awesome	orange
What is sister?	loving	gray
What is forever?	caring	yellow
What is beginning?	start	green
What is education?	learning	black
What is disability?	down syndrome	light purple
What is love?	heart	red
What is the past?	history	black and gray
What is adulthood?	adults	brown
What is time?	right now	white
What is home?	hugging	light yellow
What is daughter?	sister	violet
What is faith?	true	indigo
What is sleep?	bed	blue
What is safety?	be safe	pink
What is ending?	end	gray
What is history?	past	green
What is sadness?	happy	blue
What is the future?	the present	red
	working	light brown

GUARDIAN'S ANNUAL STATUS REPORT FOR AN ADULT

Full Name of Party Filing Document

Mailing Address (Street or Post Office Box)

City, State and Zip Code

Telephone

Email Address (if any)

IN THE DISTRICT COURT FOR THE _____ JUDICIAL DISTRICT
FOR THE STATE OF IDAHO, IN AND FOR THE COUNTY OF _____

IN THE MATTER OF THE ESTATE OF:	Case No. _____
_____	**GUARDIAN'S ANNUAL STATUS REPORT FOR AN ADULT**
an Incapacitated Person.	(I.C. §) Fee Category:
an Individual with a Developmental Disability.	(I.C. §) Fee Category:

Instructions.

This form provides the court with information about an incapacitated adult or individual with a developmental disability for whom a guardian has been appointed. This form should NOT be completed for a minor who has a guardian.

A guardian must file this report within 30 days of the anniversary date of the guardian's appointment and annually thereafter or as ordered by the court. Please answer all applicable questions thoroughly. Type or write your answers with black ink and make sure they are readable.

This report must be signed by the guardian under penalty of perjury and filed with the court. Copies must be provided to the person under guardianship's attorney and any other individuals specified by the court. Please make a copy for your records.

SECTION I - Ward's Residence.

Ward's Physical Address:_____

Ward's Telephone Number(s):

Residence: _____

Cell: _____ Work: _____

Fax: _____ Email:_____

Name of Facility or Caregiver:_____

If the ward resides in a facility, please provide a contact person's name:

Facility or Caregiver's Physical Address:_____

Facility or Caregiver's Telephone Number(s):

Cell:_____ Work:_____

Fax: _____ Email:_____

Has the ward's residence changed in the last 12 months?

    Yes   No

If yes, please explain why the ward's residence changed:_____

_____

Will the ward's residence change in the next 12 months?

    Yes   No   Unknown

If yes, please explain why the planned change in residence:

COMPLETE PART A OR B

PART A: If the ward lives in a facility, such as a residential assisted living home, an intermediate care facility, a nursing home or other home with more than three non-related residents, answer the following:

    Type of facility:

        Residential Assisted Living Home

        Intermediate Care Facility

        Nursing Home

        Other (Please Explain)

How is the facility paid for?

Do you have any concerns on the quality of care received by the ward in the following areas:

Cleanliness	Yes	No
Nutrition/Meals	Yes	No
Personal Care	Yes	No
Privacy	Yes	No
Individualized Care Plans	Yes	No
Safety	Yes	No

If you marked yes to any of the above, please explain:

Describe any restrictions placed upon the ward in the facility, such as limiting visitors or phone calls:

Who imposed the restrictions and when were they imposed:

What are the reasons for the restrictions:

Describe why this facility was chosen for the ward:

Describe the ward's satisfaction with the placement:

Do you believe the ward could live and function more independently in a different type of setting?   Yes   No
If yes, why?

If yes, have you tried to change the ward's residence?   Yes   No

If yes, was the change a success? If not, why not?

SKIP TO SECTION II

PART B: If the ward does not live in a facility covered under A, answer the following:

List other people living in the ward's home and their relationship to the ward: _____ ,

List anyone who moved into the ward's home during the last 12 months: _____

List any resident in the ward's home paid to provide any services for the ward. Please list the services provided, amount paid monthly, and the source of payment:

Name: _____   Relationship to Ward: _____

Types of Services: _____

Monthly Payment: _____   Source of Payment: _____

Does the ward live with a convicted felon?

   Yes   No   Unknown

If yes, please explain:

SECTION II - Ward's Health.

Please describe the ward's current physical health:

   Poor   Fair   Good   Excellent

If poor, please explain:

Please describe the ward's current mental health:

   Poor   Fair   Good   Excellent

If poor, please explain:

Please describe any changes (improvements or declines) to the ward's physical and/or mental health in the last 12 months:_____

_____

Please describe any medical and/or mental health treatment the ward received in the last 12 months:_____

SECTION III - Ward's Services and Activities.

Is the ward involved in selecting which care and services he/she receives?

    Yes   No

If no, please explain:

Is the ward involved in developing his/her own care or service plan?

    Yes   No

If not, why not?

Comment on the ward's ability and desire to participate in social activities, such as local events, worship services, community groups, etc.: _____

_____

_____

SECTION IV - Ward's Financial Status.

Is the ward employed?

    Yes   No

If yes, explain whether the ward has control of these wages, and if not, why not:

Provide a complete description of the ward's financial resources under the control of the guardian. If applicable, attach the most recent representative payee accounting provided to the Social Security Administration, or any other required accounting:_____

_____

Name and address of conservator, if any:____

Describe efforts to allow the ward to make decisions regarding finances and any significant changes in the ward's ability to manage financial resources: _____
_____
_____

SECTION V - Guardianship Status.
Describe significant actions taken by you concerning the ward in the last 12 months:
_____
_____

How often are you in contact with the ward _____
How often are you in contact with the service providers? _____

Describe any significant problems or unmet needs of the ward not described elsewhere:

Would you or the ward like an opportunity to discuss changing or terminating the guardianship?
    Yes   No
If yes, please explain briefly:

CERTIFICATION UNDER PENALTY OF PERJURY

I certify under penalty of perjury pursuant to the law of the State of Idaho that the foregoing is true and correct.

The undersigned, _____, guardian of _____
_____, the person under guardianship, submits this report as required by Idaho law.

Date Submitted: _____
                        Guardian's Signature

Typed/Printed Name
_____
Street or Post Office Address

_____
City, State and Zip Code

_____

Telephone Number(s)

___
Fax Number

_____
Email

Is this a change in address from your previous report?　　　Yes　　　No

CERTIFICATE OF SERVICE

I certify that on (date) _____ I served a copy to: (name all parties in the case other than yourself)

x Ward: _____ _____ _____	By mail By fax (number) By personal delivery Overnight delivery/Fed Ex
x Ward's attorney (name and address): _____ _____ _____	By mail By fax (number) By personal delivery Overnight delivery/Fed Ex
x Person(s) designated by court order (name and address): _____ _____ _____	By mail By fax (number) By personal delivery Overnight delivery/Fed Ex
x Others (name and address): _____ _____ _____	By mail By fax (number) By personal delivery Overnight delivery/Fed Ex
Typed/Printed Name	Guardian's Signature

RAW MATERIALS

_____ / DAUGHTER / SISTER

Visual elements are sourced from *Starry Night*. 1889. by Vincent van Gogh; *St. Roch Visiting the Pestilent*. 1575. by Jacopo da Ponte Bassano; *The Young Orphan at the Cemetery*. 1823-24. by Eugène Delacroix; *Mademoiselle Caroline Riviere*. 1806. by Jean Auguste Dominique; and ink drawings by my mother, my sister, and me. Other materials include black printer ink, colored paper, cardstock, acrylic paint, and googly eyes.

GUARDIAN / MOTHER / _____

Visual elements are sourced from *St. Mark Saving a Saracen from a Shipwreck*. 1562-66. by Jacopo Robusti Tintoretto; *St. Roch Visiting the Pestilent*. 1575. by Jacopo da Ponte Bassano; *The Venetian Lady's Morning*. 1741. by Pietro Longhi; *Gold Marilyn Monroe*. 1962. by Andy Warhol; and ink drawings by my mother, my sister, and me. Other materials include black printer ink, colored paper, cardstock, acrylic paint, and embroidery floss.

WARD / DAUGHTER / SISTER

Visual elements are sourced from *Dance (first version)*. 1909. by Henri Matisse; *St. Roch Visiting the Pestilent*. 1575. by Jacopo da Ponte Bassano; *The Venetian Lady's Morning*. 1741. by Pietro Longhi; *Minotauromachy*. 1935. by Pablo Picasso; *Madonna and Child* 1944. by Lauren Ford; "Hammock" 1981. by Shel Silverstein; *Alba Madonna*. 1510. by Raphael; *Madonna and Child*. 1310-15. by Giotto; *Madonna and Child*. 1440. by Fra Filippo Lippi; and ink drawings by my mother, my sister, and myself. Other materials include black printer ink, colored paper, cardstock, acrylic paint, and embroidery floss.

INTERVIEWS

Questions in the color and word association interviews were generated by me—the author—and answered by my mother, little sister, and myself to inform artistic decisions. The final word in each interview and its matching color were chosen without a prompt.

ACKNOWLEDGMENTS

Thank you to Regional Arts and Culture Council, Holly House, Spring Creek Project, and Oregon State University for supporting previous iterations of this project. Thank you to all my close readers and my teachers. To my friends and my partner. To every sister and daughter and mother.

Thank you to my communities—may I take care of you how you've taken care of me.

Paige Thomas is an award-winning writer and visual artist whose creative work has received support from the Regional Arts & Culture Council, Spring Creek Project, 21ten Theatre, and elsewhere. Some of her writing can be found in *New Delta Review, Diode,* and *Columbia Journal* while her visual work has been featured in exhibitions around Portland, OR. She received an MFA from Oregon State University. *Person Under* is her debut visual poetry collection.

www.ingramcontent.com/pod-product-compliance
Lightning Source LLC
Chambersburg PA
CBHW041806160426
43191CB00004B/68